July 2015 1

CH

Contents

A new discovery

Nearly 3,000 years ago, people discovered a metal called iron. This was the start of a time known as the Iron Age.

This is an iron ornament called a firedog. A wealthy Iron Age family used it to decorate the fireplace in their home.

Made of iron

Iron was strong. People used it to make tools, cooking pots and weapons.

Iron tools were used to dig up the ground and plant crops.

People cooked food over their fires in iron pots.

Horses had iron and leather harnesses to pull carts.

Weapons were made with iron blades.

This is an Iron Age
dagger from Spain. Its
blade has an iron cover
called a scabbard.

Part of the scabbard
is missing. This is
because very old iron
rusts away.

How was it made?

Most iron was made in a very hot oven called a furnace. A craftsman then shaped the iron. This is how a sword was made.

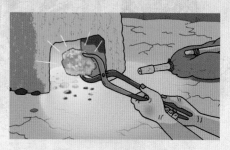

To make the furnace very hot, air was blown into it using tools called bellows.

A rock called iron ore was put into the furnace. Heating the rock made iron.

The craftsman used a hammer to shape the hot iron into a sword.

Finally, he plunged the sword into cold water. This made the iron stronger.

Craftsmen decorated iron things with glass and other metals.

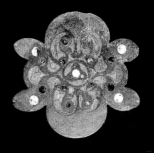

These are parts of a horse's harness. The patterns are made from stained glass and copper.

Living in tribes

Most Iron Age people lived in groups
called tribes. Different people in a tribe
did different things.

Chiefs made sure
people followed the
rules of the tribe.

People came to a
priest or priestess
for advice.

Men in each tribe
trained to be
fearsome warriors.

Most people were
farmers, growing food
and raising animals.

Craftsmen were very important people in a tribe.

They made things from iron and other metals, such as bronze, copper, gold and silver. This is a bronze ornament of a bull.

At home

Tribes built houses from materials that they found nearby.

Brochs were tall, stone towers with four floors and lots of rooms.

A longhouse had a long, sloping roof. Animals were kept in part of the house.

Crannogs were built on top of wooden posts over lakes.

Many tribes built roundhouses, like this one. Part of it has been cut away so you can see inside.

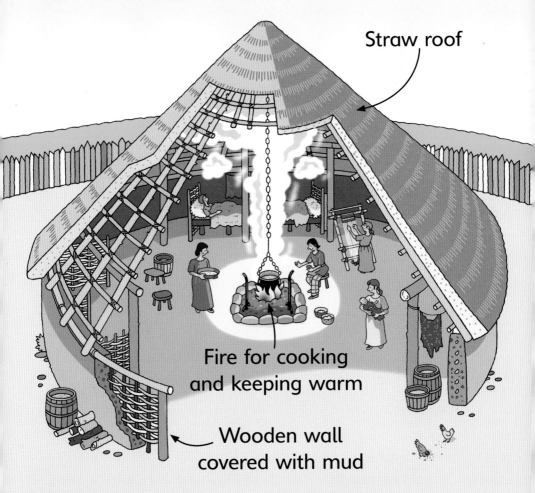

Straw roof

Fire for cooking and keeping warm

Wooden wall covered with mud

A family cooked, ate and slept in one big room.

On the farm

Most Iron Age people lived on small farms.

Men grew wheat in fields and cut them down using iron tools called sickles.

Women ground the wheat into flour, then used it to make bread.

Women and children helped to look after the farm animals.

They milked the cows, goats or sheep, then made the milk into cheese.

Trees were cut down to build houses.

People picked wild nuts and berries to eat.

Bees were kept to make honey.

Pigs were kept for their meat. They ate up any leftover food.

13

Living on a hill

Many tribes were attacked by other tribes who wanted to steal from them.

Some tribes built forts with steep banks on the tops of high hills to stay safe. These forts also showed how powerful they were.

The fort was in here.

Here are the remains of a big Iron Age hillfort called Maiden Castle in the south of England.

From the hillfort, an attacking tribe could be seen from a long way away.

Ditches and steep banks made it difficult for attackers to climb the hill.

There were only one or two entrances. These could be shut off by heavy gates.

The tribe inside the fort threw rocks and spears over the tall, wooden walls.

Dressing up

Iron Age women made clothes.

They used plants
to dye wool. Then,
they wove the
wool into cloth.

Men wore long
shirts with baggy
leggings. Women
wore long dresses.

Warm cloaks made
from sheepskin or
wool were held in
place with a brooch.

For special occasions, people put on metal bracelets and necklaces.

This is a type of necklace called a torc.

It is made from gold. Gold was very expensive, so only a rich Iron Age person would have worn it.

Iron Age people let their hair grow long and liked to try out different styles.

Fun festivals

Throughout the year, Iron Age people held many festivals. Here are some of them.

People lit fires to celebrate the first lambs being born.

Men had horse racing contests at summer festivals.

At spring festivals, cows and sheep were made to run between two fires.

People thought that this would keep the animals safe for the coming year.

At many festivals, there were huge fires and feasts. People cooked food in big pots called cauldrons.

This cauldron, from Ireland, was probably used to cook meat stews.

At one festival, people believed that the dead came back to see their friends and families.

Iron Age gods

Iron Age people believed in many gods. They gave presents to the gods to try and keep them happy.

Priests placed gifts of necklaces and weapons into a river for the gods to find.

Craftsmen made statues of the gods in the forest and put gifts next to them.

Farmers left gifts around their houses and fields for the gods, too.

This valuable silver pot is called the Gundestrup Cauldron. It was found in a bog where it had been buried as a gift.

The pictures on the cauldron are probably of different gods.

Sometimes, people or animals were killed to give as gifts.

An Iron Age funeral

Sometimes, when a very important person died, they were given a big funeral.

A dead priestess was laid on a chariot she owned when she was alive.

Members of her tribe had a big feast.

They took the body to a grave.
Then, they laid the body in it.

Food and things that the priestess owned were placed next to her.

The chariot was taken apart and placed in the grave, too. Everything was covered with a mound of earth.

Iron Age warriors

Young and fit men were fierce warriors.
They defended their homes from attack.
Sometimes, women were warriors, too.

Warriors charged
at their enemies
with iron swords
or spears.

They used wooden
shields to protect
themselves.

Some warriors wore
helmets, too.

Warriors blew trumpets, called carnyxes. These made a loud noise to scare the enemy.

Some rode on chariots.

Warriors jumped off to fight, then jumped back on.

Some warriors painted their bodies with dye and spiked their hair to look more frightening.

Words and pictures

Many Iron Age people didn't know how to read or write. Each tribe had its own bard to tell people important things.

Usually, the bard would play an instrument and sing.

He sang songs making fun of the chief's enemies.

The bard would tell everyone if the tribe won a battle.

He also sang stories about the history of the tribe.

Pictures told people different things, too.

This is a coin with a picture of someone riding a horse.

Horses were a sign of power. The craftsman who made the coin was telling people that his tribe were fearsome warriors.

How do we know?

We know about the lives of Iron Age people because experts have found and studied the things they used to own.

At a hillfort, experts remove the top layer of soil.

Very carefully, they dig into the soil until they find something.

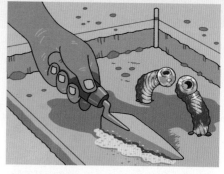

They brush off the soil, then take the item away to study it.

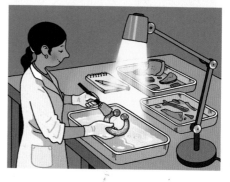

Experts have found whole bodies of
Iron Age people.

This man was
found in a bog
in Denmark.

He died over 2,000 years ago but the mud
has stopped his body from rotting away.

Glossary

Here are some of the words in this book you might not know. This page tells you what they mean.

 iron - a strong, hard metal that can be used to make many things.

 furnace - a type of oven used to make iron.

 bellows - tools to blow air into a furnace and make it very hot.

 tribe - Iron Age people who lived in the same area and did similar things.

 roundhouse - a type of house that some Iron Age people lived in.

 hillfort - forts built by tribes on hills to help them stay safe.

 bard - a storyteller and singer in a tribe who passed on information.

Websites to visit

You can visit exciting websites to find out more about the Iron Age. For links to sites with video clips and activities, go to the Usborne Quicklinks website at **www.usborne.com/quicklinks** and type in the keywords **"beginners Iron Age"**.

Always ask an adult before using the internet and make sure you follow these basic rules:

1. Never give out personal information, such as your name, address, school or telephone number.

2. If a website asks you to type in your name or email address, check with an adult first.

The websites are regularly reviewed and the links at Usborne Quicklinks are updated. However, Usborne Publishing is not responsible and does not accept liability for the content or availability of any website other than its own. We recommend that children are supervised while on the internet.

This is a statue of an Iron Age god found in the Czech Republic. People left gifts for the god around it.

Index

Acknowledgments

Photographic manipulation by John Russell
Picture research by Ruth King
Additional design by Helen Edmonds

Photo credits
The publishers are grateful to the following for permission to reproduce material:
cover © **Heritage Image Partnership Ltd/Alamy** (detail from the Gundestrup Cauldron); p1© **Peter Carroll/Alamy** (an Iron Age crannog house in Scotland, U.K.); p2-3 © **Amgueddfa Cymru – National Museum Wales**; p5 © **Dagger, Halstatt Culture, c.750-450 BC (iron), Iron Age/Musee des Antiquites Nationales, St. Germain-en-Laye, France/Bridgeman Images**; p7 © **The Trustees of the British Museum**; p9 © **Cast of a small bull figurine found in a cave of the Moravian Karst/ Werner Forman Archive/Bridgeman Images**; p14 © **Robert Harding Picture Library Ltd/Alamy**; p17 © **The Trustees of the British Museum**; p19 © **The Trustees of the British Museum**; p21 © **INTERFOT/Alamy**; p27 © **Celtic coin of horse and rider/Werner Forman Archive/ Bridgeman Images**; p29 © **Heritage Image Partnership Ltd/Alamy**; p31 © **God's Head, from the Sanctuary of Msecke Zebrovice, Bohemia (stone)/Bridgeman Images**.

First published in 2015 by Usborne Publishing Ltd., Usborne House, 83-85 Saffron Hill, London EC1N 8RT, England. www.usborne.com Copyright © 2015 Usborne Publishing Ltd. The name Usborne and the devices ♀⊕ are Trade Marks of Usborne Publishing Ltd. All rights reserved. No part of this publication may be reproduced, stored in a retrieval system, or transmitted in any form or by any means, electronic, mechanical, photocopying, recording or otherwise without the prior permission of the publisher. First published in America 2015. U.E.

Sun, moon and stars

Farm animals

Elizabeth I

Rubbish & Recycling

Dogs

Horses and ponies

Spiders

Planes

Cats

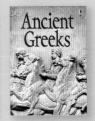
Ancient Greeks

VOLCANOES

DINOSAURS

Your Body

Armour

Sharks

Celts

VIKINGS

Castles

How flowers grow

Digging up the past

Living in space

Caterpillars and Butterflies

Ballet

Pirates

EGYPTIANS

Eggs and Chicks

ROMANS

Weather

Tadpoles and frogs

Why do we eat?

Under the sea

Bears

AZTECS

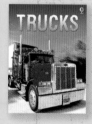
TRUCKS

Night Animals

Firefighters

Antarctica

Bugs

COWBOYS

Planet Earth

London

Seashore

China

Dangerous Animals

Rainforests

Trees

Reptiles

Ships

Bats

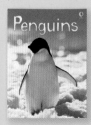
Penguins